Transform your clients' — and your own — unique dangers, opportunities, and strengths.

Deep D.O.S. Innovation is the key to identifying your clients' most important issues right now so you can provide them with unique value and support.

Your Three D.O.S. Issues

Eliminating Your Dangers

Capturing Your Opportunities

Maximizing Your Strengths

Seeing Other People's D.O.S.

Clarifying Other People's D.O.S.

Creating Your D.O.S. Future

25-Year D.O.S. Questions

Six Ways To Enjoy This Strategic Coach Book

Text **60 Minutes**	The length of our small books is based on the time in the air of a flight between Toronto and Chicago. Start reading as you take off and finish the book by the time you land. Just the right length for the 21st-century reader.
Cartoons **30 Minutes**	You can also gain a complete overview of the ideas in this book by looking at the cartoons and reading the captions. We find the cartoons have made our Strategic Coach concepts accessible to readers as young as eight years old.
Audio **120 Minutes**	The audio recording that accompanies this book is not just a recitation of the printed words but an in-depth commentary that expands each chapter's mindset into new dimensions. Download the audio at **strategiccoach.com/go/ddi**
Video **30 Minutes**	Our video interviews about the concepts in the book deepen your understanding of the mindsets. If you combine text, cartoons, audio, and video, your understanding of the ideas will be 10x greater than you would gain from reading only. Watch the videos at **strategiccoach.com/go/ddi**
Scorecard **10 Minutes**	Go to the Mindset Scorecard at the end of this book to score your Deep D.O.S. Innovation Mindset. First, score yourself on where you are now, and then fill in where you want to be a year from now. Download additional copies at **strategiccoach.com/go/ddi**
ebook **1 Minute**	After absorbing the fundamental ideas of the Deep D.O.S. Innovation concept, you can quickly and easily share them by sending the ebook version to as many other individuals as you desire. Direct them to **strategiccoach.com/go/ddi**

Thanks to the Creative Team:

Adam Morrison

Kerri Morrison

Hamish MacDonald

Shannon Waller

Jennifer Bhatthal

Victor Lam

Margaux Yiu

Christine Nishino

Willard Bond

Peggy Lam

Alex Varley

Deep D.O.S. Innovation

Each of us has our own set of *dangers* (things we're afraid of losing), *opportunities* (the possibility of gaining something), and *strengths* (our unique skills and experience). I call these our "D.O.S." issues, and I'll show you how to use them every day as your key to never-ending growth.

This also gives you a repeatable way to gain insight into what matters most to your clients and prospects, and cultivate a growth-focused relationship with them. By having a "D.O.S. Conversation" with your clients that illuminates their personal dangers, opportunities, and strengths, you make yourself an invaluable part of their future — and make your product-focused competitors seem irrelevant.

Contents

Introduction
Life's Most Important Questions
You get a handle on the daily questions that transform you and explain everyone else.

You can focus your best thinking on making progress every day by asking yourself three questions: What are my biggest *dangers*? What are my biggest *opportunities*? What are my biggest *strengths*?

I call these your "D.O.S." issues, and these questions reveal exactly how you can achieve your three most important areas of best progress for today, and then for each new day going forward—by eliminating your biggest danger, capturing your biggest opportunity, and maximizing your biggest strength.

You'll never be stuck for answers, as your emotions of fear, excitement, and confidence will reveal your biggest dangers, opportunities, and strengths. And you can use the answers that emerge as your best practical building blocks for achieving breakthrough transformations.

As soon as you can do this for yourself today, you can skillfully help others to start doing the same thing tomorrow.

Instead of competing with other people who are selling the same product or service, you'll make yourself extremely valuable to others by asking them these questions, which will help them get a handle on, and create, their futures.

Learn, don't sell.
People who are selling similar products or services in the

marketplace can essentially only outdo each other by lowering their prices. This is because in the customers' and clients' eyes, price is the only difference between the things they're being offered.

A lot of entrepreneurs claim they enjoy competition, but I've discovered that they really don't. Instead of being just another entrepreneur selling something, they want to be unique in the marketplace and have powerful, unique relationships with their customers and clients.

The D.O.S. questions get to the heart of what the other person really wants, and only they have the answers. When you ask someone a question, they can always tell when they're being sold to—when the person asking the question already has an answer in mind—and when the person asking them a question is actually interested in learning about what they think and what they want.

Secret knowledge.

In my nearly 50 years of coaching entrepreneurs, I've noticed that they all have a common goal: to have such a great relationship with their clients that they can create solutions for them based on secret knowledge—information that only they are privy to. They want to be so clear about what their best clients are aiming for that they can use that knowledge to consistently innovate new solutions for them.

And if they can keep that up, it's a permanent relationship where both sides keep getting bigger and better. The entrepreneur and the individual they're providing solutions for keep getting more successful, and with each goal and each solution, both of them become more ambitious.

Understanding, then innovation.

If your customer or client is always growing, you can count on the fact that they have three kinds of powerful emotions every day: fear, excitement, and confidence.

What they're afraid of is the *danger* of losing something and potentially moving backward instead of forward.

What they're excited about are *opportunities* they would regret not capturing.

What they're confident about are the *strengths* they've gained from previous experiences that they can maximize.

Fear is how you identify the dangers you want to eliminate, excitement is what you use to identify the opportunities you want to capture, and confidence is your guide for identifying the strengths you want to maximize.

These three emotions—fear, excitement, and confidence—are the raw material for greater progress.

Once you've figured out your own "D.O.S. issues," you can apply this system to others. Your continually deeper understanding of these three emotions of your clients and customers gives you access to the secret knowledge you can then turn into completely unique, innovative solutions that other entrepreneurs just won't be able to compete with.

The daily D.O.S.

The D.O.S. system is a way to make specific, measurable progress every day, and that progress always happens in three ways: you eliminate your biggest danger, you capture the opportunity that's most important right now, and you maximize the strength that's best suited for the job.

All three are necessary, and all three are connected to one another—you can use one to create the others. Think of them as building blocks. You can build your entrepreneurial day out of dangers, opportunities, and strengths, all of which you use your emotions to identify.

And only one danger, one opportunity, and one strength are enough for each day. You'll have more, but each day, you'll focus on transforming only the most important one in each category.

Sharing the system.
Only once you've mastered using D.O.S. for your own progress can you then gain that deeper understanding and knowledge about your clients and customers.

In the same way that you use your dangers, opportunities, and strengths to propel yourself forward, you can help your customers and clients identify their own D.O.S. issues, which will become the foundation for their progress.

In doing this, you establish a unique relationship with them that puts you entirely out of the range of competition.

For you and everyone else who learns to use D.O.S., all of this progress will be endless, because every day will present new building blocks to use, and you can innovate new solutions for the rest of your life.

THE TIME FRAME

If we were having this discussion one year from today, and you were to look back over that year to today, what has to have happened during that period for you to be happy with your progress?

Chapter 1
Your Three D.O.S. Issues
You increase your daily ability to eliminate your dangers, capture your opportunities, and maximize your strengths.

You know from lifetime experience that you have both satisfying days and frustrating days. When you look deeper, you'll see that your most satisfying and enjoyable days are the ones where you achieve certain kinds of progress.

In fact, there are three kinds of progress that, taken together, produce a sense of achievement and momentum that make you feel totally energized and motivated for the next day.

In the past, these satisfying days may have happened without your knowing why things fell into place in the right order. Now, you can consciously choose to have a satisfying and energizing experience by transforming your three most important emotional resources: *dangers, opportunities,* and *strengths*.

Dangers fill us with fear because they mean the possibility of losing something. But by thinking about them differently, you can transform dangers into *opportunities*—the possibility of gaining something.

We also have knowledge, skills, and experiences that we're very confident about. These are our *strengths*, and they're proven ways of getting results in the world.

New D.O.S. issues every day.
You can consciously use these three thinking categories to look at your experiences, eliminating fear by committing to finding a solution for a danger, and taking an opportunity and turning it into a plan for progress today. You do all this using strengths developed from past experiences, which will grow more each day.

You can start every day from now on by identifying a specific danger to eliminate, a specific opportunity to capture, and a specific strength to maximize.

The emotions of fear, excitement, and confidence are yours to use. You have a choice here. Either you allow experiences to happen to you, or you happen to experiences.

The only reason someone might not want to approach things in this way is that they're invested in placing blame on others rather than taking responsibility for how they respond to events and situations in their life.

D: Eliminating your dangers.
Dangers, opportunities, and strengths are omnipresent. Choose the most important one of each to work on each day.

The best danger to eliminate today is the one where you have the greatest fear of losing something. Take 90 seconds to list the dangers you have right now in all areas of your life. These could include the fear of losing money, health, reputation, time, and so on.

No matter how long the list is, one will always show up as your top danger for the next 24 hours. Your fear and worry will tell you what it is. And as soon as you've named and identified the fear and acknowledged that you're scared, your fear will immediately become half as strong as it was.

The actions of identifying, facing, and naming start to build your thinking capability—and thinking capability is closely followed by deciding capability, committing capability, acting capability, and achieving capability.

But unless you choose to use your fear, you never get its value.

O: Capturing your opportunities.

Next, identify your best opportunity for gaining something new that's very important to you right now. Again, this can be in any area of your life. Start by listing your current opportunities, and pick the top one, just as you did with your dangers.

Your opportunities could also be related to money, health, reputation, and time. Or perhaps they involve peace of mind, independence, confidence, happiness, or security. Just make sure they're specific.

It's important not to worry about all the other items on these lists, even though you won't be getting to them today. You're going to go through the same process tomorrow, and by dealing with the one danger, the one opportunity, and the one strength today, you're going to be changing what happens tomorrow, so you'll have to start fresh then.

You can't make a week-long schedule of opportunities to capture because your future will keep changing as you eliminate each day's top danger, capture each day's top opportunity, and maximize each day's top strength.

S: Maximizing your strengths.

The easiest and fastest way to transform today's top danger and opportunity is to maximize your best strength—the one you're always confident using.

Acknowledging that you have strengths to bring to the situation requires more courage than dealing with your dangers or your opportunities. This is because by making an inventory of your strengths, you're taking 100 percent responsibility for improving them and growing their impact.

You don't want to take your strengths for granted because then you run the risk of becoming complacent and getting stuck at a certain level of achievement. You want to be always growing and maximizing your best strengths.

Nothing's more important.

The D.O.S approach requires that you spend as much of every day as possible completely in the present. A lot of people have a hard time doing this because they're captured either by a bad past or a fearful future. But D.O.S. muscles are ones you always use in the present, eliminating fear and making measurable progress to achieve future goals.

Make the decision right now to take this D.O.S. approach over the next three days. On the morning of the fourth day, and for the rest of your life, nothing will be more successful and satisfying than going through this process.

If you start with D.O.S., anything you want to learn, you'll learn better. Anything you want to master, you'll master more quickly and to a higher degree. And anything that's interesting will become far more interesting to you.

Chapter 2
Eliminating Your Dangers
You identify and transform your single most immediate danger every day, turning it into a new capability.

Every day, each of us has fears about losing something in some area of our lives. As we look ahead to new possibilities, there are always immediate situations we're afraid or anxious about. Maybe you're worried about losing an opportunity, losing your reputation, losing a relationship, or losing access to a capability.

Dangers are the things that keep you up at night—the potential losses you want to eliminate.

One of your three most important projects for today is to choose to face your single biggest danger right now. Commit to doing everything necessary to eliminate this danger and all the fear that comes with it by the end of the day.

By the time you go to sleep tonight, it will no longer be a danger. The fear will be gone. You'll feel energized and capable. And because of today's achievement, you'll transform an even bigger danger tomorrow.

One danger every day.
It can sometimes feel like our fears of losing something are happening outside of ourselves, but the fear is all internal. And in order to get rid of our fears, we first have to recognize and acknowledge that we're afraid.

Start each day's progress and achievement by identifying what you fear most—your biggest danger—and focus on eliminating it by the end of the day.

Pushing away the fear doesn't make it go away. It gives it the chance to sneak up on you later. So use your fear. By allowing yourself to feel it, you'll get a little jolt of adrenaline, which, if managed properly, can be a force of energy.

Only you know which one.
You're the only person who knows which of your dangers is most important, because you're the only one fearing the immediate possibility of that loss.

The biggest dangers that show up for me are ones that involve teamwork. If there's something I need to do in order for someone else to take it and continue, it feels like a loss for me if I don't get my part done. Examples like this can happen almost every day.

No matter what your biggest dangers are, you'll be able to identify them by staying in touch with your emotions.

When you use your emotions productively, identifying your top danger according to your strongest fear, you can train them to show you what's really going on through how you're feeling about it. You use your brain to describe it, and you can visualize what it would feel like if you missed out on it and suffered that loss.

Eliminate by transforming.
Everyone has fears, and no, they're not pleasant things to feel, but they can be extremely useful safeguards.

Just don't let the danger stick around. Use the adrenaline from the fear it inspires to give you focus and energy. The emotion of fear is there anyway, so you might as well put it to work instead of giving it a free ride in your brain.

Instead of trying to avoid or escape from the danger, use the negative emotions of the danger to creatively produce a breakthrough.

Commit, take action, energize.
The moment you commit to transforming your single top danger by the end of the day, you're immediately able to take actions that energize you.

And you can make that commitment before you necessarily have the solution in mind. Once you've identified the danger, you can say, "I'm going to move forward on this even if I don't know right now exactly how to pull it off. I'm committing to going forward to find a solution."

You're still at least partially feeling the fear when you do this, but your mind and energies are focused.

I've given this a lot of thought and concluded that all the bad things in my life happened because I didn't tell the truth about what was happening to me emotionally.

Since I started talking to other people about this, I've discovered that everyone goes through emotional upset and that it's possible to talk yourself through it and take action.

If you ignore your emotions, you won't be fooling anyone but yourself.

Dangers become capabilities.

As soon as you transform your first danger, something remarkable happens: the fear you transformed today becomes an opportunity for a new capability tomorrow.

Every danger you've had has scared you. You could imagine something bad happening. It triggered you into action and had you make use of memories of past situations where you had done something like this before.

Those times when you've been scared, faced it, and come out the other side, you developed a new, transformative capability. And that particular situation will never scare you in the same way again.

This is where confidence comes from: having gone through an experience of fear and developing new capabilities from it.

This applies even to new situations you've never been in before, because what you *have* done before is identified a danger and then taken it and eliminated it by transforming it.

Use your emotions.

Trying to bypass your emotions creates enormous complications and complexities. And if you refuse to face your own fears, you won't like seeing that emotion in others, which limits how useful you can be to them.

You'll feel some fear every day, and every day you can use that fear to identify a danger and transform it into personal growth.

Chapter 3
Capturing Your Opportunities

You transform your single most immediate opportunity today into a teamwork achievement that multiplies your confidence.

Opportunities are always about your *future*. They're the possibility of a gain—just as dangers are the fear of a loss—and the biggest opportunities that show up for you are the ones you're most afraid of missing out on.

They're the reverse of dangers, making us feel excitement about gaining something instead of feeling fear about losing something. But you have to feel the fear of the danger in order to access the excitement of the opportunity. If you shut yourself off from one, you don't get the other.

Because you've already eliminated the day's biggest danger, getting rid of that potential for loss, you've earned the right to make even more progress by achieving the biggest gain you can today. Now you can go ahead and focus on an opportunity you're excited about.

Last night, you didn't have this achievement, but by tonight, you will. You'll feel more confident just visualizing achieving the opportunity, and you'll be even more confident later today when you've achieved it.

Fastest, easiest progress.
Once you've eliminated your biggest danger, which is the potential loss you're most scared about, it's much easier to identify today's biggest opportunity.

When you're excited about an opportunity, you can instantly feel the possibility of very fast progress, and you know that it's going to be a bigger and better achievement that will move you forward.

You get a hit of adrenaline from this potential gain because it's something you never saw before, and this feels very exciting.

Being constantly surprised by new things that are at least as good as anything you've experienced before can extend your life by making you want to keep going forever. So it's important to deal properly and carefully with these daily experiences and to arrange your life so that these exciting things can keep happening.

Biggest new gain today.

You have to be in tune with your full range of emotions in order for every part in the D.O.S. system to work, and identifying your most important opportunity to work on each day is similar to, and as easy as, identifying your biggest danger each day.

Ask yourself, "Before the end of the day, what is my easiest, fastest way to gain something important?" The one possibility that excites you most is your answer. Achieve it today.

Just as with my biggest dangers, more and more now, the opportunities that show up for me as the biggest priorities are ones where I have to get something done before handing it off to someone else to do their part on it.

It's these teamwork achievements that I've found lead to the biggest payoffs, and the payoffs are always growing.

Best teamwork project.

Identify the most exciting new gain you can have each day, and then quickly determine who can help you achieve it. Now, the opportunity gets even more exciting.

The teamwork I have with certain individuals on a constant basis has been the greatest pleasure of all work experience I've had in my life.

When I used to complete something on my own, it was interesting, but it didn't go beyond me. Teamwork takes it beyond me. It's extremely enjoyable to engage in, so my emotions are very keyed in to this total teamwork experience.

It can be difficult for some people to appreciate and reproduce this great experience even once they've had it because society places so much emphasis on individual skills, capabilities, and performance. But teamwork is how we get the biggest and best results in the most enjoyable way.

Creates a better tomorrow.

Having eliminated your danger and achieved your gain for today, you end the day on a high note, and your excitement from capturing today's opportunity automatically makes tomorrow more positive and promising.

Today is where you take action, but yesterday is what you measure against. And tomorrow, you'll have a higher measurement.

This gives you a tremendous sense of growth and prog-ress. There's a very useful by-product that comes from doing things this way. Becoming conscious about how you handle your own emotions means that you become very gifted at helping other people with their emotional responses to their own unique dangers and opportunities.

Your ability to sense, understand, and help other people with their aspirations is a function of how you deal with your own and is the single greatest skill to have in the marketplace.

Big confidence boost.
At the end of each day, you'll have eliminated the danger you were most scared about. That's a win.

On top of that, you'll have achieved measurable progress by capturing the opportunity you were most excited about.

In the cases of both the danger being eliminated and the opportunity being achieved, your actions took them from just being ideas in your mind to being reality. This means you have a repeatable creative ability, and you'll be feeling a big boost of confidence.

You can see the confidence boost in children when they first start standing up and taking their first steps after many attempts.

If you can retain the excitement you got from achieving wins when you were a child, and keep that feeling through-out your lifetime, in a certain sense, you never get older.

Chapter 4
Maximizing Your Strengths
You continually expand your appreciation of the unique strengths you already have that can be used in today's new situations.

Every day, you feel more capable because every day, you develop new strengths. You may not have realized this before, but when you reflect on the dozens of dangers and opportunities you've successfully transformed in the past, you'll see that it's absolutely true.

As soon as you have this realization, you acquire a permanent confidence, knowing that your best strengths are always available to make you more successful today.

And where is that confidence most needed? When facing your top danger and biggest opportunity each day.

But at those stages, the strength isn't real yet, not until you take the fear of a loss and transform it by eliminating the danger, or take the excitement of a gain and transform it by capturing the opportunity. Then, your strength and confidence grow.

That strength is now available for you to use in taking on more challenging dangers and opportunities that require even more capability. And you can use your built-up confidence even in situations you've never faced before.

Every day, more capable.
When it comes to eliminating each day's danger and

capturing each day's opportunity, you're going to use a specific, already developed skill, one you've used before in completely different situations and that has grown as a result of those experiences. In using your strengths this way, they become even stronger.

So what's happening is, every day, you transform the day's new further achievement into capabilities that will make you more successful in responding to tomorrow's new challenges and possibilities.

Uniquely yours.
You're not drawing on some kind of generic strength when it comes to eliminating dangers and capturing opportunities. The strength you use is one you've used before in other situations and that you've already strengthened through use.

Like your dangers and opportunities, your growing strengths are unlike those of anyone else. Every time you transform a unique experience, your new strengths are uniquely yours.

And the more you use the D.O.S. system, the more you'll recognize other people doing the same thing—transforming their own unique dangers and opportunities, and developing their own unique strengths.

You'll feel a resonance with such people, and you'll share a language with them to talk about your progress. They're on the same path as you and will immediately understand you and your process.

So D.O.S. is not only a strategy for daily personal growth, it's also a language for communicating with other people who use the same approach.

Appreciating specific wins.

The only way we can measure progress is backward. Only by looking back to where you started can you really appreciate how much further ahead you are now.

So each night, when you've successfully checked off the day's danger, opportunity, and strength, you'll be able to measure exactly what progress you've made. You'll feel stronger than you felt that morning, and you'll be further ahead than you were the night before.

You can take your specific achievements, where you used your best skills to transform negatives into positives, as proof that you'll be able to accomplish even more tomorrow.

You can live this way your whole life, focusing just on what progress you can make during 24-hour periods. You don't have to worry about a week from now, or next month. The next 24 hours are all that ever matter.

You'll be able live in the present, and the emotional rewards you'll receive from doing three significant things each day—identifying them and taking the actions to accomplish them—will bring enormous depth and satisfaction to your daily life.

Tonight, you're stronger.

You'll start each day with the confidence that no matter what surprising new challenges and opportunities emerge, you'll handle them in new ways that make you stronger.

Every day is different, but your way of making progress each day is the same, and you can always be confident, knowing that the process works in all kinds of situations.

Commitment and courage.

The two greatest strengths you can always have at the start of each new day are the commitment to improve and the courage to succeed.

Everyone wants to have increased capability and confidence, but not everyone wants to put in the work to achieve them. When you're faced with a new challenge, you don't yet have the capabilities to handle it, so you have to start by making a commitment. You might not yet know exactly how you're going to do this, but you commit to moving forward. And you do so using courage.

The difference between courage and confidence is that confidence feels good, and courage doesn't. When you use courage, you're moving forward and doing what you have to do, but because you don't yet have the capability, you don't have confidence yet either.

This becomes part of your daily consciousness, where you know you're going to have to go through the phases of commitment and courage for part of the day in order to create greater capability and confidence. That awareness becomes its own strength with which you can tackle any danger, take advantage of any opportunity, and maximize any strength.

The greatest strength you can have is knowing how to create capability and confidence in any situation.

Chapter 5
Seeing Other People's D.O.S.
You use your deepening understanding of your own dangers, opportunities, and strengths to appreciate the D.O.S. of others.

Achieving clarity about your own D.O.S. issues is just the first step toward even greater progress that lies ahead of you. Now, there's a bigger jump: seeing the D.O.S. issues of everyone else around you.

One of the things I've learned from nearly 50 years of coaching entrepreneurs is that everyone always has some kind of danger—a fear of losing something—on their mind. I suspect it's a human condition, but it's especially true of people who are goal-focused.

Someone who is always envisioning a bigger future for themselves will be scared of missing an opportunity to achieve a goal and of potentially losing their current position and moving backward.

And if someone doesn't know that eliminating dangers and capturing opportunities are related to maximizing their strengths, they won't know to apply skills they already have to the issues on their mind.

Deepening understanding.
As you become more skillful at using your dangers, opportunities, and strengths to organize and transform each day, you'll quickly recognize how other entrepreneurs can use the D.O.S. system in their own lives to continually move forward.

One common danger for entrepreneurs is getting even more ambitious just as others start retiring. When an entrepreneur reaches a certain age, their contemporaries will start talking about plans to end their careers and focus on other things, while the entrepreneur wants to continue achieving bigger and better goals in their field. The entrepreneur will stand out, and quite possibly feel isolated, for wanting to keep going.

This is why communities of entrepreneurs are so important. When you're part of an entrepreneurial community, everyone is of the same mindset regarding never wanting to retire. You're united in your love of your work and your excitement about it, and know there's no need to explain this to the others. It's very powerful to be part of a group where your mentality and aspirations are considered normal.

Start with your D.O.S.

Sharing the D.O.S. system with another person involves going through a process of thinking and questioning, but you can't lead someone else through it unless you're first completely clear about the process yourself. That's why you have to get a handle on eliminating your own dangers, capturing your own opportunities, and maximizing your own strengths.

Once you know how D.O.S. works for you, you can switch your attention to others around you, using your understanding of your own D.O.S. issues to identify what they're dealing with.

You know it works from using it in your own life, and you'll see how it can work just as well for everyone else who learns it from you and applies it to their own dangers, opportunities, and strengths. It mutually reinforces the system when you see how well it works for both yourself and someone else.

Seeing they're the same.

The D.O.S. framework provides a simple and clear perspective for understanding how you can help others focus their thinking.

When circumstances change and plans get disrupted, one of the best things you can do for people is teach them about D.O.S., walking them through identifying their biggest dangers to eliminate, most important opportunities to capture, and most valuable strengths to maximize. I call this The D.O.S. Conversation.

This focused discussion helps them restore their vision of the future, which might have been interrupted as a result of unforeseen events.

You can say, "Well, you've lost a bit of the future you'd planned. So, let's not just restore your future but make it even bigger than it was."

Unique fears, excitement, and confidence.

You'll grow more and more skilled at guiding other people's thinking so they can make decisions and take actions that will transform their unique fears, excitement, and confidence.

You know that D.O.S. works for you, so you can trust that the same process will work for others. Once you get the basics of the process down, you really can't do it wrong. It's vital to keep The D.O.S. Conversation focused on the other person, because only they can say what their biggest fears are and what they're most excited about, just as you're the only one who can answer those questions for yourself.

And if someone is unwilling to answer the D.O.S. questions, it could be that they're either mistrustful—The D.O.S. Conversation quickly cuts through to what's most important to them—or else they haven't actually created a future in their own mind, so they really don't have answers to your questions.

Your D.O.S., their D.O.S.

All of the complexity and confusion we feel about the future becomes remarkably simpler when we share our daily D.O.S. progress with each other.

Every person has countless thoughts and experiences that no one else is privy to. But there are ways we've learned to cooperate with one another and make progress together, and conversation is one of the greatest teamwork skills human beings can have.

It's incredible to think about how, despite all the things we don't know about each other's lives, we can sketch out a structure and path for how we're going to achieve certain things for ourselves, and some things together, using teamwork.

And it's all facilitated by a great conversation.

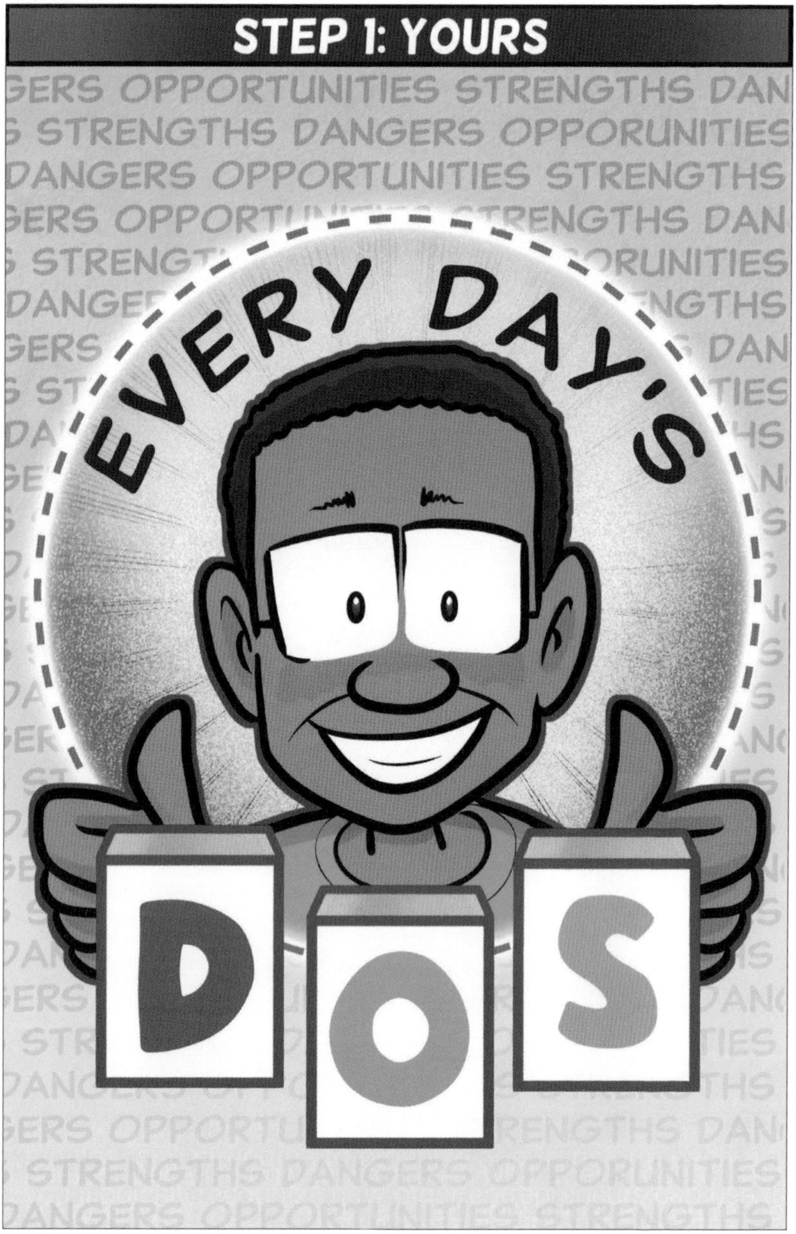
STEP 1: YOURS
EVERY DAY'S
DOS

Chapter 6
Clarifying Other People's D.O.S.

You easily help other people clarify their D.O.S. issues — and they're quickly able to create a bigger and better future.

Your growing ability to transform each day's most important danger, opportunity, and strength suddenly opens up a whole new capability to quickly and easily help other people do the same.

Everyone faces their own unique D.O.S. issues every day, but until you empower them to think in these terms, they're unaware of this. The moment you help them, they can immediately start creating a new, better future.

We feel things emotionally before our brains get to work on thinking about them, and you'll find that every person whom you ask the D.O.S. questions will be able to consciously identify their biggest dangers, opportunities, and strengths once they're looking for them.

The three questions—*What danger do you feel the most fear about? What opportunity do you feel most excited about?* and *What strength do you have that could be used to eliminate the former and capture the latter?*—are what's needed for them to use their emotions to make a plan for progress. The questions help them focus on what's most important right now and forget about everything else for the moment.

Your daily D.O.S. skill.

As you identify your most important danger, opportunity, and strength daily and take immediate action to transform them before the end of the day, you'll continually increase your skill.

There are two main reasons most people don't do this:
1. They haven't made the commitment to doing it, and
2. They engage in this type of thinking only in emergencies or when something extraordinary is going on.

But just as with physical exercise, you can't expect to get the full benefit of this process or to become really good at it by doing it just once or on occasion.

This is an ordinary activity that each of us can do every day to stay clear about our D.O.S. issues and become more skillful at helping others clarify their own. I've been consciously using D.O.S. like this for about 30 years, and it's always worked for me.

I don't find anything more fundamental or essential than these three questions. In my years of asking them, I haven't found anything that goes deeper or gets to the heart of the matter in the way these questions do.

Easy, but not obvious.

Anyone can acquire this same daily D.O.S. skill, but it's not obvious to them until you show them how you do it for yourself.

I've never encountered anyone dedicated to learning this who couldn't learn it quickly, and I've never met anyone who learned it and wasn't spectacularly happy about gaining this skill.

There's no downside here. Other people become clearer about their futures thanks to your questions, and you automatically grow as a result of using your skill to help them.

Instantly understandable.
As soon as you ask someone about their specific danger, opportunity, and strength for today, their thinking immediately transforms and they can see how to make improvements.

Explain to them how you divide things into three piles—the fear pile, the excitement pile, and the confidence pile—and then let them do the rest, identifying which danger, opportunity, and strength are showing up for them as the most important.

All you're doing is asking them to think about their thinking and providing a framework for them to do that. The questions you're asking are open-ended, and only they know the answers. You can't know them, because you don't have their emotions.

It's important in this process that you show no judgment about their feelings and goals. Respect that they know what the answers are.

Specific actions for today.
Once the other person has identified their three D.O.S. issues, ask them what actions they can take today to eliminate the danger, capture the opportunity, and maximize the strength.

By guiding their thinking in this way and setting up the structure, you're providing leadership and direction they're likely not getting anywhere else.

Every day, they're faced with an abundance of options and information, and by taking them through this clarifying process, you're setting aside the space for them to get very specific about the actions they can take right now to get "unstuck" and move forward with confidence.

Three actions, new future.
You'll discover that every time you have The D.O.S. Conversation with a new person, it produces the same gratifying result where they immediately see and create a new future.

I never hold anyone to anything they say they're going to do. This is because sometimes The D.O.S. Conversation helps them determine everything they *don't* want to think about, and now they can move on to what they really want to think about.

So your job in that situation is just to help them clear out the stuff that isn't important for them right now, allowing them to go ahead and do something totally different.

The value is in the conversation, giving them the opportunity to think about their thinking and helping them to organize it and come up with specific actions. But whether they follow through is 100 percent up to them. And the conversation itself may have served the purpose of simply clearing their minds so they could focus on what was really important.

Don't hold any judgment about whether they do what they say. You'll see their energy completely transform in the moment, and you'll know they've received a great gift.

Chapter 7
Creating Your D.O.S. Future
You use the expanding power of D.O.S.-based communication and collaboration to create a growing transformative community.

Members of the D.O.S. community are outliers. We don't experience the same general fears that others do. We only highlight specific, unique fears, which we then eliminate, followed by capturing specific opportunities and maximizing specific strengths. In this sense, we're flowing with the stream while other people are getting hit by the tsunami.

Think of D.O.S. as the common language of the community—first, as a way for you to communicate about your future, and second, as a way for others to communicate about theirs.

Dangers, opportunities, and strengths. A very simple language and framework that lets you and others talk about anything that lies ahead.

This comprehensive communication then enables you to collaborate with a growing community that thinks about its D.O.S. future. Members of this community grow while recognizing one another's growth. And if one member gets off track and is struggling as a result, others will remind them to get back on the D.O.S. path.

Secret D.O.S. password.
D.O.S. is like a secret language that allows you to communicate with a constantly growing number of individuals who

are enthusiastically committed to daily growth. The reason why it's a secret is that most people would never think of having The D.O.S. Conversation with themselves, let alone with someone else. Society puts an emphasis on celebrity and on being interesting to other people, but the nature of engaging someone in The D.O.S. Conversation means being *interested* in the other person.

In a D.O.S. community, there's no competition to be the star. Each individual supports and assists in the others' growth while using the same formula to achieve their own growth.

Everyone in the community shares this connection, and there's mutual admiration and respect. This is the complete opposite of a community in which each person is striving to be better than everyone else, as is so often the case outside of the D.O.S. community.

You share, they grow.

You know the process works for you and for everyone else anytime you choose to organize a particular day on the basis of transforming a specific danger, opportunity, and strength.

So when you share this skill with someone, that person grows. Once you've gone through the D.O.S. questions with them, ask them if going through the process was a positive experience. You can then suggest that they go out and pass that good feeling on to others, sharing their new D.O.S. skill so that even more individuals can experience that growth.

Good-willed people have a desire to be useful and to enhance other people's lives, even though we don't tend to learn this skill in our society. So the sharing and growing will always continue.

They share, you grow.
In our greater society, where everyone is learning more or less similar things, it can be hard to get a sense of your individual impact.

But when someone you've had The D.O.S. Conversation with comes back and tells you what they've accomplished and how much clarity they now have, you'll get a strong sense of the help you provided for them.

And as the individuals you've shared the D.O.S. secret with go on to share it with others, you'll grow from the endless new ways they're transforming their own lives. You'll learn from the various positive results that have come from new people learning the secret, and that's one way in which everyone in the D.O.S. community is always getting smarter.

Because every person's dangers, opportunities, and strengths are unique, there's no end to the unique ways of effectively using D.O.S. And there's no end to the community being able to learn from not only their own, but others', experiences.

D.O.S. collaboration.
Everybody's daily D.O.S. transformation automatically leads to effortless collaboration with one another that multiplies every time someone learns the secret.

The best kinds of collaborations are ones where you combine your Unique Ability—what you love to do and do best—with someone else's in a way that's never been done before in order to create value for a particular type of client or customer.

An ideal collaboration is one where each of you is putting your different capabilities toward transforming the D.O.S. issues of the same audience. You both have an understanding of D.O.S., and you can imagine the exponential value creation impact you'll have by putting your capabilities together toward the same goal.

This is how you achieve 10x or 100x the result. It's not about money—it's about combining unique capabilities. Money is the by-product of a value-producing collaboration.

There's no comparison or competition involved, only cooperation. The world of the D.O.S. community expands for everyone in it.

Endlessly expanding.

Your daily D.O.S. achievement and progress multiply everyone else's D.O.S. breakthroughs, and other people's daily D.O.S. achievements and progress result in your capabilities continually expanding.

As I get older, my aspirations grow, but it becomes easier to achieve them because I'm not alone. When I was alone, it was hard, but more and more, I've become part of a community in which there are massive amounts of good will, support, and understanding among all of its members.

It's incredibly enjoyable—I'm always discovering brand new things and being pleasantly surprised by other people's experiences. And I know there's no end to how far this community can take all its members. It's just going to keep expanding.

Chapter 8
25-Year D.O.S. Questions

You master — over the next 25 years — ever more insightful D.O.S. questions that uniquely transform your marketplace relationships.

In the past, you spent a lot of time looking outside of yourself for the secrets to achieving faster and easier success. But now, you see that the secret is actually inside of you— inside your own dangers, opportunities, and strengths.

The more you discover and explore your own D.O.S. issues, the more you can identify and help other people transform their futures.

You'll become so fascinated and motivated by this single creative activity that you'll find it easy to do for the next 25 years, leading to new breakthroughs, exceptional collaborations, and innovative solutions.

The R-Factor Question.

As part of your D.O.S. Conversation, there's another important question to ask: "If we were having this discussion one year from today, and you were to look back over that year to today, what has to have happened during that period for you to be happy with your progress?"

I call this The R-Factor Question (the R stands for *relationship*). It lets you know if the person you're talking to sees a future with you. Other than the D.O.S. questions themselves, it's probably the most important question you can ask someone because it's open-ended and allows the person answering to really take a look at themselves in the future.

Answering the question means they have to not only imagine themselves in the future, but also having a future discussion with you. So to proceed, they have to know you're a safe person to talk to. To an extent, this question forces them to make a decision about their relationship with you.

It also puts them in a position to think in two time frames: the current one, in which they're creating their answer, and the future one, in which they'll be looking back to now.

The phrasing "happy with your progress" is important because you're not asking them what makes them happy in general, but what they'll be happy about having accomplished by that future date. They're the only person who can answer the question because they're the only person who can know what progress will make them happy.

They're literally creating their own future.

The past is done and the present is now, so the only place you can create value for someone is in their future. Asking them The R-Factor Question makes it possible for them to create a new, bigger future in their mind. And you're the trusted witness to their new vision.

When we're asked questions, it's often by someone who already has an answer in mind. But this question is one you can't have an answer for and one they've probably never been asked before.

Being asked the question gives them an incredible opportunity, and as long as they're someone who imagines having a bigger future, they'll come up with answers, whether it's immediately or somewhere down the road.

Dangers, opportunities, and strengths.

You're in control of the structure of the conversation, but the person you're talking to is completely in charge of the answers.

You want them to answer with specifics, not generalities. You're asking them specifically what dangers need to be eliminated, what opportunities need to be captured, and what strengths need to be maximized for them to be happy with their progress one year from now.

You know from your own experience of being asked these questions what's required to come up with the answers: they have to use their fear to determine their most important dangers, their excitement to identify their most important opportunities, and their confidence to figure out their most important strengths. You can help guide them, but only they can know the specific answers.

First D.O.S. game plan.

With the D.O.S. questions, you not only help someone see their future in a new way, you also enable them to create a practical plan for transforming their most immediate D.O.S. issues.

You can't have a practical plan without a time frame. That's why when you ask The R-Factor Question, you say, "If we were having this discussion one year from today ..." If the person says that they can't see that far ahead, you can change the time frame to six months from now or another appropriate time frame. You could even extend the time frame to three years in some cases. The point is that you're looking at a particular amount of time.

Their answers also have to be measurable. They have to be about specific dangers to eliminate, specific opportunities they want to capture, and specific strengths they want to maximize, all connected to specific emotions, so that they know it—and feel it—when they've been accomplished.

There has to be no doubt, one way or the other, as to whether these have been achieved by the date in question.

When you have a time frame, an intended result, and a way of measuring whether the results have been achieved, you have a game plan.

25-year mastery.
As you keep having this discussion with each of your important relationships, it will keep getting more exciting— so exciting, in fact, that you'll want to do it more and more over the next 25 years.

Twenty-five years from now, where do you think you'll be after that many years of empowering all of your relation-ships with the D.O.S. questions and helping everyone who's important to you to be happy about their progress and excited about their future?

You'll get better at having The D.O.S. Conversation every time you do it. Engaging others in The D.O.S. Conversation, including asking The R-Factor Question, will make you feel relevant and connected, and you'll be rewarded for it. You'll be praised for your contribution, you'll be referred for it, and you'll end up being highly paid for it.

Conclusion
Deep D.O.S. Innovation
You initiate all new value creation in your future based on deeply understanding other people's emerging D.O.S.-based aspirations.

You're at a point where it's automatic to think and talk about your future and others' futures in terms of dangers, opportunities, and strengths. Because of this deeply embedded daily habit, you're always creating entirely new practical solutions that enable everyone to make progress that transforms new D.O.S. issues in remarkably unique ways.

The future of every human being includes dangers, opportunities, and strengths. Knowing this is a great way to feel commonality with every other person on the planet.

Over the course of your lifetime, you'll get to know a sizable number of individuals, and D.O.S. is a way of establishing common ground in these relationships very quickly.

You'll be able to determine right away if someone wants to speak the common language of D.O.S., and you won't waste your time or energy on those who aren't interested in collaboration.

D.O.S. is everyone's future.
Every person wants something, and what they want is unique to them because of the unique experiences they've already had. You can't really know what someone wants until you have a conversation with them about their dangers, opportunities, and strengths.

You've transformed your entire way of looking at the future, seeing it now as a creative process of deeply understanding everyone's progress in terms of eliminating dangers, capturing opportunities, and maximizing strengths.

Each of us experiences freedom and growth to the degree that we can personally identify our specific desires and goals. Only then can we receive the support of other people's capabilities to help us get there.

There's no general game plan for human beings—there's just the combined total of each person identifying and working on their own aspirations.

Competition-free innovation.

Your approach to daily value creation originates from collaborating with the D.O.S.-based aspirations of others, not by competing with other value creators.

People who compete want their future to "beat" other people's futures. But that's based on the idea that there's a limited amount of future out there that people can get a hold of.

The mistake is thinking that there's no future outside of your own aspirations. I've coached thousands of entrepreneurs, and each one's aspirations are unique. The only way I can be useful to them is by engaging with their future, helping them achieve their goals and vision.

And the best way I've found to do that is by asking good questions that produce good answers.

I'm always looking for new, useful questions that make me more skillful at helping people identify the actions they need to take to achieve their goals and to identify the team-work they need to engage in.

The more skillful someone gets at asking these questions of themselves and others, the more connected that person feels with the community. So more and more, my aspirations include other people's aspirations.

Endlessly emerging aspirations.

It's kind of magical that within a conversation that lasts maybe an hour, we humans can envision an entirely different future simply by becoming aware that the person we're talking to has a capability that can be combined with ours to create something new.

Having The D.O.S. Conversation with someone forces you to focus on that individual, so you always feel the fascination and motivation that comes from discovering something unique, something you've never seen before.

Every time I have The D.O.S. Conversation, I discover something unique and my D.O.S. skills expand because my aspirations for the future are connecting to someone else's. That always leads to new innovations, and there's no end to this daily process of discovery and creativity.

D.O.S. issues never end. They're always emerging because each individual's aspirations are endless.

You can always be participating in this growth-driven process, and it will always be getting bigger and better. But you can never own it, because it involves everybody together.

You transform, they transform.
You transform your future by understanding your D.O.S. issues, and with your guidance, leadership, and direction, others will increasingly transform their own D.O.S. issues. Then they, in turn, will be able to help other people transform *their* D.O.S. issues.

More and more, I'm making positive connections with people. Every day, I expect to be struck by something brand new, and I have a sense of tremendous growth of human creativity and innovation. And it's all because I'm following the D.O.S. process.

Richly, uniquely unpredictable.
Every day is unique. Every day, you have the possibility of exploring someone's aspirations. It just keeps getting better, and life will never get boring.

The more experience you have in structuring these conversations with others, the more wisdom you'll have with which to respond to their answers, even though their answers will always be surprising. You'll learn to expect to be surprised by the answers, but you'll still appreciate their uniqueness. Your ability to draw out and appreciate people's uniqueness will continually grow.

Making D.O.S. a personal habit, having that framework, and getting comfortable with the emotions of fear, excitement, and confidence allows you to have future-based and rich conversations with other people. And the more you do it, the more mastery you have, which leads to mutual transformation, and it's always richly and uniquely unpredictable.

The Strategic Coach Program
For Ambitious, Collaborative Entrepreneurs

You commit to growing upward through three transformative levels, giving yourself 25 years to exponentially improve every aspect of your work and life.

"Deep D.O.S. Innovation" is a crucial capability and a natural result of everything we coach in The Strategic Coach Program, a quarterly workshop experience for successful entrepreneurs who are committed and devoted to business and industry transformation for the long-term, for 25 years and beyond.

The Program has a destination for all participants—creating more and more of what we call "Free Zone Frontiers." This means taking advantage of your own unique capabilities, the unique capabilities around you, your unique opportunities, and your unique circumstances, and putting the emphasis on creating a life that is free of competition.

Most entrepreneurs grow up in a system where they think competition is the name of the game. The general way of looking at the world is that the natural state of affairs is competition, and collaboration is an anomaly.

Free Zone Frontier

The Free Zone Frontier is a whole new level of entrepreneurship that many people don't even know is possible. But once you start putting the framework in place, new possibilities open up for you. You create zones that are purely about collaboration. You start recognizing that collaboration is the natural state, and competition is the anomaly. It makes you look at things totally differently.

Strategic Coach has continually created concepts and thinking tools that allow entrepreneurs to more and more see their future in terms of Free Zones that have no competition.

Three levels of entrepreneurial growth.

Strategic Coach participants continually transform how they think, make decisions, communicate, and take action based on their use of dozens of unique entrepreneurial mindsets we've developed. The Program has been refined through decades of entrepreneurial testing and is the most concentrated, massive discovery process in the world created solely for transformative entrepreneurs who want to create new Free Zones.

Over the years, we've observed that our clients' development happens in levels of mastery. And so, we've organized the Program into three levels of participation, each of which involves two different types of transformation:

The Signature Level. The first level is devoted to your *personal* transformation, which has to do with how you're spending your time as an entrepreneur as well as how you're taking advantage of your personal freedom outside of business that your entrepreneurial success affords you. Focusing on improving yourself on a personal level before you move on to making significant changes in other aspects of your life and business is key because you have to simplify before you can multiply.

The second aspect of the Signature Level is how you look at your *teamwork*. This means seeing that your future consists of teamwork with others whose unique capabilities complement your own, leading to bigger and better goals that constantly get achieved at a measurably higher rate.

The 10x Ambition Level. Once you feel confident about your own personal transformation and have access to ever-expanding teamwork, you can think much bigger in terms of your *company*. An idea that at one time would have seemed scary and even impossible—growing your business 10x—is no longer a wild dream but a result of the systematic expansion of the teamwork model you've established. And because you're stable in the center, you won't get thrown off balance by exponential growth. Your life stays balanced and integrated even as things grow around you.

And that's when you're in a position to transform your relationship with your *market*. This is when your company has a huge impact on the marketplace that competitors can't even understand because they're not going through this transformative structure or thinking in terms of 25 years as you are. Thinking in terms of 25 years gives you an expansive sense of freedom and the ability to have big picture goals.

The Free Zone Frontier Level. Once you've mastered the first four areas of transformation, you're at the point where your company is self-managing and self-multiplying, which means that your time can now be totally freed up. At this stage, competitors become collaborators and it becomes all about your *industry*. You can consider everything you've created as a single capability you can now match up with another company's to create collaborations that go way beyond 10x.

And, finally, it becomes *global*. You immediately see that there are possibilities of going global—it's just a matter of combining your capabilities with those of others to create something exponentially bigger than you could ever have achieved on your own.

Global collaborative community.

Entrepreneurism can be a lonely activity. You have goals that the people you grew up with don't understand. Your family might not comprehend you at all and don't know why you keep wanting to expand, why you want to take new risks, why you want to jump to the next level. And so it becomes proportionately more important as you gain your own individual mastery that you're in a community of thousands of individuals who are on exactly the same journey.

In The Strategic Coach Program, you benefit from not only your own continual individual mastery but from the constant expansion of support from and collaboration with a growing global community of extraordinarily liberated entrepreneurs who will increasingly share with you their deep wisdom and creative breakthroughs as innovators in hundreds of different industries and markets.

If you've reached a jumping off point in your entrepreneurial career where you're beyond ready to multiply all of your capabilities and opportunities into a 10x more creative and productive formula that keeps getting simpler and more satisfying, we're ready for you.

For more information and to register for The Strategic Coach Program, call 416.531.7399 or 1.800.387.3206, or visit us online at *strategiccoach.com*.

THREE LEVELS OF

FREE ZONE FRONTIER

25	26	27	28
29	30	31	32
33	34	35	36

10X AMBITION

13	14	15	16
17	18	19	20
21	22	23	24

SIGNATURE

1	2	3	4
5	6	7	8
9	10	11	12

FREE ZONE

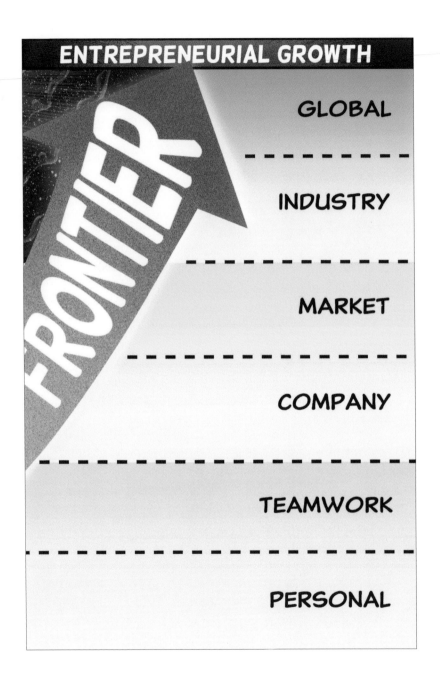

The Deep D.O.S. Innovation Scorecard

Turn the page to view the Mindset Scorecard and read through the four statements for each mindset. Give yourself a score of 1 to 12 based on where your own mindset falls on the spectrum. Put each mindset's score in the first column at the right, and then add up all eight and put the total at the bottom.

Then, think about what scores would represent progress for you over the next quarter. Write these in the second scoring column, add them up, and write in the total.

When you compare the two scores, you can see where you want to go in terms of your achievements and ambitions.

Mindsets	1	2	3	4	5	6
1 Your Three D.O.S. Issues	You have always felt like a victim of your daily circumstances, never having developed a way of understanding what's happening.			You're tired of being emotionally reactive to your negative situation and are now committing to learning how to respond in creative ways.		
2 Eliminating Your Dangers	You've always felt you have so many dangers surrounding you that it's impossible to think about anything else except escaping them.			You realize it's time to start facing your dangers because you won't make any progress until you start dealing with them directly.		
3 Capturing Your Opportunities	You start each day dreading what lies ahead. Yesterday was bad, so you don't see how today can be any better. No plan for tomorrow.			You realize that you have new opportunities every day, and now you have to improve your ability to focus on one of them at a time.		
4 Maximizing Your Strengths	You always see yourself as lacking and deficient. At the same time, you resent the capabilities and skills of everyone around you.			You're completely clear that you can't be someone else, and you're now committed to identifying and strengthening your own skills.		
5 Seeing Other People's D.O.S.	You've never been conscious of why you feel the way you do about anything. Things just happen to you, and you don't understand any of it.			You've tried to grasp how other people look at their lives and futures because you want to act in a way that's useful to them.		
6 Clarifying Other People's D.O.S.	You are so bogged down with your own uncertainties and problems that you've never given any thought to helping other people with theirs.			You've come to a fundamental insight that you can't transform your own situation unless you help other people with theirs.		
7 Creating Your D.O.S. Future	You're not really into communicating or collaborating with others, which is why you always end up isolated, frustrated, and failing.			You've tried all kinds of theories and techniques to be more successful, but D.O.S. is the first one you can improve every day.		
8 25-Year D.O.S. Questions	You never earn more than a survival income over your lifetime because you have no understanding of other people's aspirations.			You realize that trying to sell without understanding other people's aspirations doesn't work. You're willing to start using D.O.S.		
Scorecard	➡	➡	➡	➡	➡	➡

7	8	9	10	11	12	Score Now	Score Next
You've learned how to attach yourself to the slogans and strategies of much smarter people who seem to handle things well.			You increase your daily ability to eliminate your dangers, capture your opportunities, and maximize your strengths.				
You've spent your whole life conforming within groups of people who protect you from your dangers — because you can't protect yourself.			You identify and transform your single most immediate danger every day, turning it into a new capability.				
You've worked your whole life to benefit from achievers who create new opportunities for you, without any effort on your part.			You transform your single most immediate opportunity today into a teamwork achievement that multiplies your confidence.				
Your lifetime habit has always been to attach yourself to other people's superior capabilities, never working on your own.			You continually expand your appreciation of the unique strengths you already have that can be used in today's new situations.				
You've achieved a successful way of dealing with other people based on the belief that everybody has the same goals in life.			You use your deepening understanding of your own dangers, opportunities, and strengths to appreciate the D.O.S. of others.				
You've worked steadily to achieve security and certainty in your own life and feel that other people's worries and concerns are their business.			You easily help other people clarify their D.O.S. issues — and they're quickly able to create a bigger and better future.				
You've reached a point of comfortable success and status where you don't see the point of learning any new approach.			You use the expanding power of D.O.S.-based communication and collaboration to create a growing transformative community.				
Your entire life until now has been one of successfully being involved in providing the right products and services to the right clientele.			You master — over the next 25 years — ever more insightful D.O.S. questions that uniquely transform your marketplace relationships.				

About The Author
Dan Sullivan

 Dan Sullivan is the founder and president of The Strategic Coach Inc. and creator of The Strategic Coach® Program, which helps accomplished entrepreneurs reach new heights of success and happiness. He has over 40 years of experience as a strategic planner and coach to entrepreneurial individuals and groups. He is author of over 30 publications, including *The 80% Approach*™, *The Dan Sullivan Question*, *Ambition Scorecard*, *Wanting What You Want*, *The 4 C's Formula*, *The 25-Year Framework*, *The Game Changer*, *The 10x Mind Expander*, *The Mindset Scorecard*, *The Self-Managing Company*, *Procrastination Priority*, *The Gap And The Gain*, *The ABC Breakthrough*, *Extraordinary Impact Filter*, *Capableism*, *My Plan For Living To 156*, *WhoNotHow*, *Your Life As A Strategy Circle*, *Who Do You Want To Be A Hero To?*, *Free Zone Frontier*, *Always Be The Buyer*, *Simplifier-Multiplier Collaboration*, *Total Cash Confidence*, and *Scary Times Success Manual*, and is co-author with Catherine Nomura of *The Laws of Lifetime Growth*.

Printed in Great Britain
by Amazon

26454974R00048